ELEMENTARY CATECHISM

on the

CONSTITUTION

of the

UNITED STATES

For The Use of Schools

by

ARTHUR J. STANSBURY

BOSTON:
HILLIARD, GRAY, LITTLE, AND WILKINS
1828

ISBN 978-1-60386-609-5

DIGITALIZED BY
WATCHMAKER PUBLISHING

District *of* Massachusetts, To Wit:

District Clerk's Office

Be It Remembered, that on the 3d day of November, A.D. in the fifty-second year of the Independence of the United States of America, Milliard, Gray, Little, and Wilkins, of the said district, have deposited in this office the title of a book, the right whereof they claim as proprietors, in the words following, to wit:

"Elementary Catechism on the Constitution of the United States. For the Use of Schools. By Arthur J. Stansbury. "In conformity to the act of the Congress of the United States, entitled, "An act for the encouragement of learning, by securing the copies of maps, charts, and books, to the authors and proprietors of such copies during the times therein mentioned", and also to an act, entitled "An act supplementary to an act, entitled, 'An act for the encouragement of learning, by securing the copies of maps, charts, and books, to the authors and proprietors of such copies, during the times therein mentioned', and extending the benefits thereof to the arts of designing, engraving, and etching historical and other prints."

JNO. W. DAVIS,
Clerk of the District of Massachusetts,

J. B. Russell, Printer

Preface

That a people living under a free government which they have themselves originated should be well acquainted with the instrument which contains it, needs not to be proved. Were the system, indeed, very cumbrous and extensive, running into minute detail, and hard to be retained in the memory, even this would be no good reason why pains should not be taken to understand and to imprint it upon the mind; but when its principles are simple, its feature plain and obvious, and its brevity surpassing all example, it is certainly a most reprehensible negligence to remain in ignorance of it. Yet how small a portion of the citizens of this Republic have even a tolerable acquaintance with their own Constitution? It has appeared to the author of the following sheets that this culpable want of acquaintance with what is of such deep interest to us all, is to be traced to the omission of an important part of what ought to be an American education, viz. the study of the civil institutions of our country. We prize them, it is true, and are quite enough in the habit of boasting about them; would it be well to teach their elements to those whose best inheritance they are.

The following work has been prepared with a view to such an experiment. It is written expressly for the use of boys and girls, and it has been the aim and effort of the writer to bring down the subject completely to a level with their capacity to understand it. Whether he has succeeded the trial must show. He has purposely avoided all abstruse questions, and has confined himself to a simple, common-sense explanation of each article. It is very possible some inaccuracies may be discovered; and should this be the case, they shall be carefully corrected, should the work be so far approved as to reach another edition.

In the mean time he cannot but indulge the hope, that in laying this little offering upon the altar of our country, he has rendered her an acceptable service.

Elementary Catechism

Question. In what country do you live?
Answer. In the United States of America.

Q. Why is this country called the 'United States of America'?
A. Because it is made up of a number of States which were once separate, but afterwards agreed to unite together.

Q. What do you mean by a State?
A. I mean any district of country whose people are all under one government.

Q. Had then the different States which united together, each a government of its own?
A. Yes; but they agreed to put themselves all under one general government.

Q. Why did they do this?
A. Because it would promote their general welfare.

Q. Is some government necessary in every country?
A. Certainly; without it nobody would be safe: not only our property, but our lives would be in danger.

Q. Cannot all the people of a country govern themselves?
A. If every man was perfectly virtuous, and knew what would be best for himself and others, they might. But this is far from being the case; and therefore the people of every country are and must be governed.

Q. How is this done?
A. Laws are made which all must obey; whoever disobeys them is punished.

Q. Who makes these laws?
A. They are made in different ways, under different governments. In some countries a single man make the laws according to his own pleasure.

Q. What is such a government called?
A. A Despotism, or absolute monarchy: and the person who thus rules is a Despot, or absolute monarch. In other states a certain number of persons belonging to ancient or wealthy families make the laws.

Q. What is such a government styled?
A. An Aristocracy or oligarchy. In other cases the people themselves meet to make the laws. This is called a pure Democracy.

Q. A state must be very small where all the people can meet in one assembly.
A. This form of government is only suited to a small city, or rather village, and can never take place in a state of any extent. One other form remains; that is, where the people, too numerous to meet, themselves, choose certain of their own number to meet for them. This is called a **Representative Government**, because those who meet represent all the rest. It is also called a **Republic**.

Q. Which of these ways of governing a nation is the best?
A. The last. A country thus ruled is said to be free, or to enjoy liberty: but where a single man may make what laws he pleases, and all the rest must obey him, the people are no better than slaves.

Q. Why do they obey him?
A. Because he has an army of soldiers whom he pays, and who force the people to obedience.

Q. Cannot they raise an army too, and resist him?
A. This has sometimes been done, and after much bloodshed and confusion, the people have partially succeeded; but they have more frequently failed, and then they were more oppressed than before.

Q. How is this country governed?
A. It is a Republic, and is governed by persons whom the people choose from time to time to make the laws.

Q. Was it always a Republic?
A. No. The states were formerly Colonies.

Q. What do you mean by Colonies?
A. When a part of the people of a nation remove to some distant place, where they settle, but still continue to be governed by the nation from which they came out, these new settlements are called Colonies, and the country which governs them is called the mother country.

Q. By what nation were the American Colonies governed?
A. By Great Britain. Most of the people who first settled this country came from England, Scotland or Ireland, (which three countries make up Great Britain) and long after they had settled here, continued to be governed by laws, most of which were made in England.

Q. Were these laws good and wise?
A. Many of them were; and for a time the colonies were perhaps better off than if they had entirely governed themselves, because, though Great Britain did rule them, she also gave them protection by her fleets, and did many things for their advantage. But afterwards very unwise and unjust laws were made, and such as threatened to destroy all liberty in the colonies.

Q. What did the colonies do then?
A. They made complaints, and reasoned for a long time with Great Britain, trying to persuade her to act more justly.

Q. Did Great Britain listen to their complaints and repeal those bad laws?
A. No but instead of that sent over ships and soldiers to force us to obey them.

Q. And did we obey?
A. No; the people of the colonies consulted with each other what was to be done, and at length took up arms, raised such armies as they could, and though they had few soldiers, no experienced officers, and but little money, they carried on a war against the whole power of Great Britain, and having (with aid from France) forced two British armies to lay down their arms and surrender themselves prisoners, they at length compelled Great Britain to acknowledge their independence.

Q. What do you mean by that?
A. I mean that she was compelled to consent that all those colonies, which had before been governed by laws made for them by her, should after that have liberty to make laws for themselves, and obey her no more.

Q. When we speak of this war, what do we call it?
A. We call it the American Revolution.

Q. What do you mean by a Revolution?
A. A revolution means some great change of government; and we ought ever to remember ours with ardent gratitude to God for so great a blessing, and with lasting love and reverence for those good, wise, and brave men, who went through such dangers and sufferings that their country might be free.

Q. When and where did the war of the revolution begin?
A. At Lexington and Concord, villages near Boston in Massachusetts, on the 19th of April, 1775.

Q. How long did the struggle continue?
A. More than seven years.

Q. When did it end?
A. On the 21st of January, 1783 when a treaty was signed at Paris acknowledging the independence of the United States.

Q. Why is the 4th of July kept with such public rejoicing through all parts of the United States?
A. Because on the 4th of July, 1776, the Colonies first declared themselves free and independent; from that day the independence of the country is reckoned in all our public proceedings; though it was not acknowledged by Great Britain until 1783.

Q. What was the change produced by the Revolution?
A. The different Colonies became each a free STATE, having power to govern itself in any way it should think proper.

Q. Had not one state any power over the other?
A. None at all and the several states might have remained entirely distinct countries, as much as France and Spain.

Q. Did they?
A. No. Having been led to unite together to help each other in the war, they soon began to find that it would be much better for each of them that they should all continue united in its farther prosecution, and accordingly they entered into an agreement (which was called a Confederation) in which they made some laws which they all agreed to obey; but after their independence was obtained, finding the defects of this plan, they called a Convention in which they laid a complete plan for uniting all the states under one **General Government**; this plan is called **The Federal Constitution**. On this great plan, or Constitution, the safety and happiness of the United States does, under Almighty God, mainly depend: all our laws are made by its direction or authority; whoever goes contrary to it injures and betrays his country, injures you, injures me, betrays us all, and is deserving of the heaviest punishment. Whoever, on the contrary, loves and keeps it sacred, is his country's friend, secures his own safety, and furthers the happiness of all around him. Let every American learn, from his earliest years, to love, cherish and obey the Constitution. Without this he can neither be a great or a good citizen; without this his name will never be engraved with honor in the pages of our history, nor transmitted, like that of Washington, with praises and blessings to a late posterity.

Q. You say that in a republic the laws are made by certain persons whom the people choose for that purpose: who make the laws in our republic?
A. The laws which concern only one of the states are made by persons chosen by the people of that state, and who, when met, are called the Legislature, the General Assembly, or the General Court, of that particular state. Those, for instance, who make laws which concern only the state of New York, are called the Legislature of the state of New York; those who make laws which concern only the state of Massachusetts, are called the General Court of Massachusetts. But laws which concern all the states or more states than one are made by the **Congress of the United States**.

Q. But if even the Congress itself should make a law which is contrary to the Constitution, must the people obey it?
A. No.

Q. Who is to determine whether any law is contrary to the Constitution or no, the people themselves?
A. No: but certain persons whom they have appointed, (called Judges of the Supreme Court of the United States.)

Q. Do the members of the Congress of the United States all meet together in one assembly, when they make the laws?
A. No: they meet in two separate assemblies, one of which is called **The Senate**, and the other is called **The House of Representatives**.

Q. Who chooses the persons who shall be members of the House of Representatives?
A. The people of all the different states: because the laws of Congress concern all the states, and must be obeyed by all the people of this Republic.

Q. Have boys a right to choose them?
A. No, boys are too young.

Q. Are any other persons unfit?
A. Yes.

Q. How is it determined who may, and who may not choose them?
A. By the laws of each state. Whoever is allowed to choose the members of the Legislature of any state, is also allowed by the Constitution to choose members of the House of Representatives of the United States. Some states allow one class of persons to choose and other states allow a different class each state acts as it thinks best. This choice is called an Election.

Q. How is it conducted?
A. On a day fixed beforehand, and publicly known, the people who are to choose, and who are called voters, meet at certain places called the Polls: here persons sit called Inspectors, who have certain boxes called ballot boxes before them, and each person who votes puts into a hole in the top of these boxes a piece of paper with the names of the persons whom he chooses written or printed on it. These pieces of paper are afterwards examined and counted by the Inspectors, who keep a written account of the names voted for, and the number of votes given by the people for each. The persons having the greatest number of votes are chosen. There are some slight differences in the mode of holding elections in the different states, but it is the same in every important particular.

Q. Are the times, places, and manner of holding these elections fixed by Congress?
A. No: They have, thus far, been left to be regulated by each state for itself, but Congress may fix them if it thinks fit.

Q. Suppose a dispute should arise concerning an election, and one person shall declare that he has been fairly chosen, while another denies it, and insists that he himself has been chosen; who has power to settle the dispute?
A. A dispute between persons who claim a seat in the House of Representatives can be determined only by the House of Representatives; a dispute between persons claiming a seat in the Senate can be settled by the Senate only. Such disputes frequently arise.

Q. When a person is chosen to be a Member of the House of Representatives, how long does he continue so?
A. For two years.

Q. When the two years have expired, may he be chosen again?
A. Yes.

Q. Suppose he dies before the time is out?
A. Another is chosen in his stead, for the rest of the time.

Q. How old must a person be before he can be chosen a Member of the House of Representatives?
A. Twenty-five years old.

Q. May a person be chosen who has just come into the United States, and who is a subject of some other country (that means, who is bound to obey the laws of some other country)?
A. No. Any person, to be chosen a Member of our House of Representatives, must either have been born in the United States, or must have been naturalized seven years before he is chosen.

Q. Naturalized? What does that mean?
A. A person who was born in another country and comes to live in this, is not owned as a citizen of the United States till he has lived among us a certain time; and then, (after knowing something of our laws and customs), has taken a solemn oath to obey the government. He is then admitted as a citizen of our republic. This is called his naturalization; and when once naturalized, he is allowed to choose the rulers, and do all other things, the same as if he had been born among us.

Q. May the people of one State choose a person who is an inhabitant of another State to be a Member of the House of Representatives?
A. No; he must live in the State where he is chosen.

Q. How many persons may be chosen by each State, as Members of the House of Representatives?
A. The number of Representatives of any State is in proportion to the number of people in that State. At present every forty thousand people send one Representative; but this has been, and may be, altered, with the increase of the number of people.

Q. Some of the States have large numbers of slaves living in them, and others have many Indians; are these counted in making up the forty thousand?
A. No; three fifths of the number of slaves is allowed, that is every five slaves are counted as if they were three free persons: those Indians who pay taxes, (that is, who pay money for the expenses of governing and defending us) are counted; those who do not pay taxes are not counted.

Q. How is it known what number of people each State contains?
A. Certain persons are appointed to count the people and take a written list of them. Such a counting is called a census, and it takes place once in every ten years. (In the year 1790 the United States contained 3,929,326; in 1800, 5,309,758; in 1810, 7,239,903; and in 1820, 9,638,166.)

Q. When the Members of the House of Representatives meet to make the laws, are they all equal, or does anyone preside over them?
A. They choose one of their own number, whose duty it is to preside over them while they are met to do business, and to see that they proceed in a regular and orderly manner in doing their public duty. He is called their Speaker. They also choose a person who is not one of their own number to keep a written account, from day to day, of all that is done by them while assembled. That written account is called a Journal of the House of Representatives, and the person who keeps it is called the Clerk of the House. They also choose another person who is called their Sergeant-at-Arms and who may, when so ordered by the House, seize any Member who disobeys the rules, or who is charged by the House with any crime, and imprison him. They also choose another person as their Door Keeper

who is to take care that no person be admitted into the hall where the Representatives are sitting, but such as are permitted by law. These several persons, thus chosen, are called the Officers of the House of Representatives, and remain in office two years.

Q. Who choose the Members of the **Senate of the United States**?
A. The Legislature of each State chooses the Senators for that State.

Q. How many Senators may there be?
A. Two from each State.

Q. When a citizen is chosen by the Legislature of his own State to be a Member of the Senate of the United States, how long does he continue such duty?
A. For six years. If he dies before the expiration of that time, or resigns his office, (that is,if he declares it to be his wish not to be a Senator any longer) another is appointed in his place.

Q. Are all the Senators chosen at the same time, as Members of the House of Representatives are?
A. No. Only one third are chosen at once two years afterward another third is chosen and two years after that, another third, so that every two years one third part of the Senators go out of office; but the same persons may again be chosen if the Legislatures who chose them before wish to send them again; if not, they send others in their place.

Q. How old must a person be before he can be chosen a Senator of the United States?
A. Thirty years old.

Q. Can he be chosen if he has not been born in the United States?
A. Yes, if he has become a citizen by being naturalized, and has been a citizen for nine years.*

Q. Can a Senator for one State be chosen by the Legislature of another State?
A. No. The Legislature of each State must choose its own Senators, from persons residing in its own bounds.

Q. Does the Senate choose a Speaker, as the House of Representatives does?
A. No. The person who is chosen by the people to be Vice President of the United States,is made, by the Constitution, President of the Senate; his duties are like those of the Speaker of the House of Representatives, except that he is not obliged to keep order in debate. Their other officers are the same in all respects, as those of the House of Representatives, and are chosen by the Senators in the same manner.

Q. Do the Senators ever sit as Judges?
A. Yes. When any civil officer of the United States (that is, not an officer of the army,) is guilty of a violation of his public duty, he is accused, or charged, by the House of Representatives, and tried by the Senate, Such an accusation is called an Impeachment.

Q. What do you mean by his being tried by the Senate?
A. The Senators take a solemn oath that they will carefully attend to the proof that shall be brought before them, and according to that proof declare the accused person innocent or guilty, as the case may be. The House of Representatives appoint some of their own Members to lay the proof before the

Senate, and afterwards the accused person lays before them the proofs in his defence; when both have been heard, the Members of the Senate vote, that is, each one declares his opinion; and if two thirds of all the Senators who are present declare the accused person to be guilty, he is adjudged guilty; if not, he is declared not guilty.

Q. Cannot the Senate, in like manner, impeach that is, solemnly charge an officer before the House of Representatives?
A. No. None can bring an impeachment but the House of Representatives, and none can try an impeachment but the Senate.

Q. What is the consequence if the Senate declare an officer of the United States to be guilty?
A. He may be turned out of office, and prevented from ever again holding any office of honor, trust, or profit, under the United States government.

Q. May he be further punished?
A. Not by the Senate. He may afterwards be tried before a Court of Law, and punished in the same manner as any other criminal for offences against the law.

Q. May ever the President of the United States be thus impeached and punished?
A. Yes. In this free and happy country no man is so great as to be above the law. The laws are supreme; to them all persons, from the President of the United States to the poorest and the meanest beggar, must alike submit. This is our glory. Let every youthful American exult that he has no master but the law; let him mark the man who would change this happy state of

things as the enemy of his country; and above all let him remember that as soon as he himself breaks the law, he becomes himself that enemy.Whoever violates the law helps to weaken its force, and, as far as he disobeys, does what in him lies to destroy it: but he who honors and obeys the law strengthens the law, and thereby helps to preserve the freedom and happiness of his country. In some governments it is held that "the king can do no wrong", here we know no king but the law, no monarch but the constitution: we hold that every man may do wrong; that the higher he is in office,the more reason there is that he be obliged to answer for his conduct; and that as a great officer, if treacherous, is a great criminal, so he ought to be made to suffer a great and exemplary punishment.

Q. How often does Congress meet?
A. It must meet once, at least, in every year; but may meet oftener if necessary.

Q. Is any day fixed for its meeting?
A. Yes; the first Monday in December; but it has power to alter that to some other fixed day. When Congress ceases to meet, it is said to Adjourn.

Q. Suppose all the members of the Senate, or all the members of the House of Representatives do not attend a meeting, can those who do attend make laws without them?
A. If more than one half are present, they have in most cases power to do whatever the whole number could have done. More than one half are called a Majority, less than one half are called a Minority. As many as are necessary to do business are called a Quorum.

Q. Supposing less than one half should attend, can they do nothing?
A. Yes, they have power to send for the others and compel them to attend. If they do not choose to do this, they have power to adjourn till the next day; (that is, they may separate after agreeing to meet the next day) and so they may continue to do till a Quorum shall be present to do business.

Q. Are there any fixed rules for doing business in Congress?
A. Certainly, every thing is done by settled rules, called Rules of Order.

Q. Who settles what these rules shall be?
A. The Rules for the Senate are made by the Senate; the Rules for the House of Representatives are made by the House of Representatives. Each House has power to alter its own Rules of Order; or to suspend them, that is to say, a particular rule may be disobeyed for a certain time; after which it is again in force.

Q. Suppose a Member refuses to attend, or behaves, when he does attend, in a disorderly manner?
A. He may be punished in any way the other Members think proper.

Q. May he be even expelled from the House? that is, turned out of it?
A. Yes, but not unless two thirds of all the Members think he deserves it.

Q. You said that the Clerk of the House of Representatives keeps a written Journal of all that is done in that House; is a Journal kept in like manner by the Secretary of the Senate?
A. Yes.

Q. Are these Journals published, that is, printed and sold?
A. Yes; excepting such parts as either House of Congress may think proper to keep secret for a time, when the public good requires it.

Q. Does the Congress ever sit in secret?
A. Yes. Whenever they are engaged in business which it will be better for the public good to keep secret for a time, they close their doors. At other times they sit in public, and everybody who can get into the gallery may see and hear all that is done.

Q. Does the Journal show how each Member voted in every case that came to be considered?
A. No. But if one fifth of the Members present when any measure is proposed, require that the names of those who voted for and against it, be put down in the Journal, it must be done.

Q. After Congress has met, may either House adjourn (that is, cease to meet) for more than three days at a time, without the consent of the other House?
A. No.

Q. Do the two Houses, that is, the Senate and House of Representatives, meet in the same building?
A. Yes.

Q. May either House remove to any other place?
A. No, not unless the other House removes too.

Q. Do Members of Congress receive any thing for doing the business of the public?
A. Their chief and best reward is the honor of serving their country; but as many of them cannot afford to leave their own business so often and so long without having the loss in some measure made up to them, the Constitution says that they shall be allowed a compensation to be ascertained by law, and paid out of the Treasury of the United States.

Q. Who fixes the rate of compensation, that is, how much the Members shall have?
A. It is fixed by Congress.

Q. Ought they to be allowed to fix their own wages?
A. It cannot be avoided; the rate must be fixed by law, and there is none who have power to make law for this country but the Congress only.

Q. May Members of Congress be arrested, (that is, seized by a sheriff or constable) for debts they owe, while they are attending to their public duty?
A. Their duty is of so much value to us all that the Constitution will not allow them to be arrested while going and returning from their home to the place where Congress meets,nor while they are attending there, except in three cases.

Q. What are these?
A. If they have been guilty of treason, felony, or breach of the peace.

Q. When is a person guilty of treason?
A. When he makes war against the United States (that is, when he endeavors by force to overturn or to resist the Government,) or when he helps or comforts others who are

making war against them. But this must be proved by at least two witnesses, who have both seen him do some act of treason. The crime is punished in any way Congress thinks fit; and they have determined that it shall be punished by death.

Q. If Members of Congress while engaged in debate, that is, in arguing about any law that is proposed to be made, shall sat any thing offensive to another Member, may he be sued for it by the other in a Court of Law?
A. No (lest this should destroy the freedom of debate, and make the Members afraid of speaking their thoughts with honesty and plainness in matters for the public good,) a Member cannot be called to account in any other place for any thing he says upon the floor of Congress.

Q. May Members of Congress be appointed to any civil office under the United States?
A. Not while they continue to be Members; if they are appointed to any office and wish to accept the appointment, they must give up their seats in Congress; nor can they be chosen Members again while they hold the office.

Q, Supposing Congress creates any new office, (that is, appoint some public duty to be done and allow the person who does it a compensation) or shall increase the pay before allowed for doing the duties of any office, that is already established, may any Member of the Congress which did this be appointed to such office?
A. No, not till the whole time for which he was chosen a Member shall have expired.

Q. How does Congress proceed in making the laws of the land?
A. A Member usually proposes that some other Members, called a Committee, shall consider whether it will not be proper to make a law for some particular matter, which he explains. If a majority of the Members think it will be best to consider of the matter, they order certain Members to do so. These Members, or Committees, meet together, and having considered the proposal, determine whether it is proper to advise the Members of the House to make a law respecting it. If they think it is they put down in writing the words of such a law as it will be best to make. This writing is called a Bill. They then return to the House, and either in writing or by word of mouth, declare what they have done, and state the reasons for it. Such, a statement is called a Committee's Report. The Bill is then read twice. The Member who first proposed the matter now farther proposes,(or Moves, as it is called) that this Bill be considered by all the Members. If this is agreed to, the Bill is then taken under consideration. Every Member has an opportunity to propose such alterations in it, as he pleases; and every Member may give reasons why such a law ought or ought not to be made. If any alterations are made, the Bill as altered is written over again and read a third time; when, after full consideration, it is passed, that is, finally agreed to.

Q. Is it now a law?
A. By no means. The Bill thus passed by one House is then sent to the other House.There it is again considered, and, if the House thinks proper, is further altered. It is then returned to the House where it began. If this House disapproves of the alterations made by the other, it sends the Bill back, that that House may give up the alterations but if they will not give them up, then a Committee of Conference is appointed; that is, certain Members are sent from each House to meet together,

and try to bring the matter into such a form that both Houses will agree to it; if they succeed, and the Houses agree, the Bill is then Engrossed, (that is, copied in a fair hand) on parchment, and signed by the President and Secretary of the Senate, and by the Speaker and Clerk of the House of Representatives.

Q. Is it now a law?
A. Not yet. The engrossed Bill is then sent to the President of the United States for his approbation; if he approves it, he signs and returns it; the Bill then is called an ACT, and becomes the law of the land.

Q. What if he does not approve it?
A. If he does not approve it, he must return the Bill together with his objections, in writing, to the House in which it began; that House must copy the whole of these objections into their Journal, and then consider the Bill once more. When they have done this, if two-thirds of that House shall agree to pass the Bill, they must send it, together with the President's objections to it, to the other House. There the Bill must, in like manner, be reconsidered; and if two thirds of this House also agree to pass it, it becomes a Law. But in all such cases, the names of all the Members of each House who voted for and against the Bill, must be put down in the Journals.

Q. Suppose the President of the United States should neglect to sign and return a Bill sent to him by Congress?
A. If he does not sign or return any Bill within ten days after it is sent to him (not counting Sundays), it becomes a Law, unless in that time Congress shall have ceased to sit.

Q. Is not this a better way of making the laws of the Country, than either of those we first considered?
A. It is hard to conceive how greater care could be taken that no wicked, unjust,oppressive, hasty, or unwise Law should pass. There is full time to consider whatever is proposed; such fair opportunity to oppose it, if wrong, and improve it, if imperfect; so many persons, and from so wide a space of country must agree in approving it, that it is scarcely possible any thing very injurious can be enacted; or, at least, if it is, that a different form of Government would have prevented it.

Q. Are there not some evils which attend this mode?
A. Nothing of human contrivance is wholly free from some defect or other; and, in time of war, when the public danger is great, and it is needful that Government should act, not only wisely, but rapidly; some disadvantage may be found to arise from so deliberate a method of passing every Law. But it is far better to put up with this, than to lose the precious blessing of so free and safe a mode of Legislation.

Q. You have said that no Laws can be made for the United States, but by Congress; may Congress make any Laws they please?
A. No. Their power is limited by the Constitution; that is, they have no power, but what the Constitution says they have. It must always be remembered, that the States, when they united to form the General Government, had full power to govern themselves; and that they gave up only a part of their power, for the general welfare. Whatever power, therefore, is not given by the Constitution to the General Government, still belongs either to the State Governments, or to the people of the United States.

Q. What power is given to Congress, by the Constitution?
A.Congress has power to do the following things: It may "lay and collect Taxes, Duties, Imposts, and Excises."

Q. What do you mean by these different terms: What is a Tax?
A. A Tax means a sum of money which the people are directed to pay, to support the Government, and defense of the Country.

Q. What are Duties?
A. Duties are sums of money, which must be paid by persons who bring goods of any kind from another country, into the United States, and which are in proportion to the quantity or value of such goods. It is paid at certain places called Custom-houses, and is sent from these to the Treasury of the United States.

Q. What are Imposts?
A. Imposts are sums of money which must be paid to the Government, by persons owning vessels, which enter the harbors of the United States, in proportion to the size of the vessels. An Impost is a duty on vessels.

Q. What are Excises?
A. Excises are sums of money which must be paid to the Government, by persons who make certain articles within the United States, in proportion to the quantity or value of the articles manufactured.

Q.What do you mean by laying these, and what by collecting them?
A. Laying a Tax, is determining how much it shall be; and collecting a Tax, is obliging the people to pay it.

Q. Could any Government long exist without this?
A. No. Every Government must have large sums of money, to use for the public good, and this is the proper way of getting it.

Q. Ought the people to complain of having to pay Taxes and Duties?
A. Certainly not; because they all receive the benefit. If nobody would pay Taxes,nobody could be defended by armies, fleets, or forts; nobody could be paid, for making or for executing the laws; the whole country would soon be without law, safety, or order;and we should all be miserable. Whoever, therefore, cheats the Government of its duties, does in reality cheat himself and his neighbor, and acts like the enemy of his country.

Q. May one part of the United States be required to pay at a greater rate than the rest?
A. No; all Duties, Imposts, and Excises must be uniform throughout the United States.

Q. What other power has Congress?
A. To borrow money on the credit of the United States

Q. What do you mean by that expression, "on the credit of the United States"?
A. It means that the people of the United States are bound to pay whatever money Congress borrows for their use. [Such money is called a Loan; and whoever lends it to the Government, receives a printed paper, acknowledging that such a sum has been lent,and promising to pay a smaller sum yearly, as Interest for the use of it. Such printed certificates are called Stock; they may be bought and sold the same as any other article,and whoever holds them when the interest becomes due, may demand, and must receive,it. If the printed

paper promises to pay six dollars a year for every hundred dollars borrowed, it is called "United States six per cent Stock"; if it promises to pay four dollars a year for every hundred, then it is called "United States four percent Stock".

Q. What other power does Congress possess?
A. It may make rules according to which the Commerce of the citizens of the United States with other nations (that is the exchange of our goods for theirs, or for money, by means of vessels or other conveyances) shall be carried on; also the commerce of one of the states with another, and that of the different states, or of the United States, with the Indian tribes. (Some persons believe that the power to regulate Commerce among the several states includes the power to make Roads and Canals from one state to another; others deny this.)

Q. What is the next power given to Congress by the Constitution?
A. You recollect what was before said about naturalization, which means the admitting of a foreigner (that is, a native of some other country) to become a citizen of the United States: Congress has power to make one uniform rule according to which this shall be done throughout the country. It may also make uniform Laws for the whole Union on the subject of Bankruptcy.

Q. What is bankruptcy?
A. When a man has not money or goods enough to pay his debts, he is a Bankrupt; and the being in that situation is Bankruptcy. The object of Laws on this subject is to compel such a man to give up all he has got to the people he owes, and to fix the terms on which he may be set free from the debts he cannot pay.

Q. What else may Congress do?
A. It may coin money; that is it may mark or stamp certain pieces of metal in a way which shall make them pass, in buying and selling, at a set value. It may also fix what shall be the value of coin that has been marked or stamped in any other country, when it is used in the United States. It may likewise declare one uniform size for the weights and measures used throughout our country.

Q. May any persons who please coin money?
A. No, none but those employed to do so by Congress (they work at a place called the mint).

Q. If any other person shall coin money in his own name, or shall stamp it so as to resemble that coined at the mint, or that which, though coined in other countries, is allowed to pass as money in the United States, may he be punished?
A. Yes; it is a crime, called counterfeiting, and may be punished in any manner Congress shall appoint.

Q. Suppose they counterfeit not the money of the United States, but the stock issued by Government?
A. They are punished the same as if they had counterfeited money.

Q. What other power belongs to Congress?
A. They may "establish Post Offices and Post Roads".

Q. What is a Post Office?
A. A place where Letters carried from one part of the country to another, at the expense of the United States, are received and delivered.

Q. And what is a Post Road?
A. A road on which the bag containing these letters (called the mail), is carried.

Q. What is meant by establishing these?
A. Making a law which directs where the Post Offices shall be, and by what roads the mail shall be carried. Some persons say that it includes a power to erect buildings for post offices, and to make roads where they are wanted; others deny this.

Q. Has Congress any farther powers?
A. It may grant what are termed Patent Rights and Copy Rights.

Q. What does this mean?
A. When a person has found out some new and useful contrivance, Congress may give him an exclusive right to make and sell what he has contrived, for a certain number of years; during that time nobody else may make or sell that article without leave from the man who contrived it, and if they do they are liable to be punished. This is called a Patent Right. Whoever writes a book may also have the exclusive right to print and sell it for a certain time; this is called a Copy Right.

Q. Can Congress erect Courts? That is, make a Law directing that a Judge shall sit at certain places, at certain times, before whom Causes or Criminals shall be tried?
A. Yes, it may appoint as many Courts as it thinks fit; but they must all be inferior to the great Court of the country, called the Supreme Court of the United States.

Q. Can it punish Piracy? That is, robbery committed at sea?
A. Yes, and all other crimes committed there; it can also punish offences against the law of nations.

Q. What do you mean by "the law of nations"?
A. I mean those rules which are agreed upon among all nations (except those who are savages) to regulate their conduct towards each other.

Q. Has Congress any other power?
A. Yes, it has one most solemn and important power, the power of Declaring War between the United States and any other nation.

Q. When Congress has declared the United States to be at war with any particular country, can any of the citizens of the United States remain at peace with that nation?
A. No; however much they may dislike the war, or love the nation against whom it is declared, all must, when required, aid in it, by their money or their services, and bring it as soon as possible to a successful end. If they attempt to aid the enemy, or forcibly hinder the success of the war, they commit treason.

Q. When the United States have cause of complaint against another nation, and yet do not wish at once to go to war, is there any other measure they can take to compel that nation to do them justice?
A. Yes. Congress may "issue Letters of Marque, and Reprisal".

Q. What are they?
A. They are certain public letters directed to merchants of the United States, who have been injured, and have been refused redress, permitting them forcibly to take vessels belonging to

the offending nation, sufficient to make up the loss; but this must be done only according to certain Rules, fixed by Congress.

Q. You say Congress may declare War; can they raise Armies; that is, can they hire soldiers to fight for the country?
A. They can; and pay, clothe, and feed them, at the public expense.

Q. Can they make a law, setting apart money enough at one time, to pay and support the army for more than two years?
A. No, not at one time; lest a wicked Congress might, by keeping up an army, remain in power beyond the time for which they were chosen, and so destroy the liberty of their country.

Q. Why was the time limited to two years?
A. Because every two years a new Congress may be chosen.

Q. Can Congress in like manner, provide and maintain a Navy? That is, buy or build ships of war; and hire, clothe, and feed men to navigate and fight them?
A. Yes; and make Rules to govern both Army and Navy.

Q. Has the Country no other defense to depend upon but hired soldiers?
A. Yes, the people themselves, who are of a proper age to bear the fatigues and hardships of War, are obliged to bear arms and defend their Country when need requires; they are called the Militia.

Q. When may they be called out, to do this?
A. When they are wanted, to enforce the laws; to overcome any of their fellow citizens,who are so foolish and wicked as to rebel against our free and excellent form of government; or to meet and drive out an enemy who invades; that is, forcibly enters any part of our Country.

Q. But as the great mass of the people are ignorant of the art of War, how is this to be done?
A. Congress has power to provide for their being taught, by collecting and arranging them in companies, and regiments, under their own officers; supplying them with arms,and causing them to be properly exercised in their use.

Q. May Congress command them, or are they to be commanded by their own State Governments?
A. The President may command so many of them us are employed in the service of the United States, the rest are commanded by the States.

Q. Who appoints the Officers of the Militia?
A. The State Governments; they also train, that is, exercise and instruct the men; but this must be done according to Rules fixed by Congress.

Q. Have you mentioned all the powers of Congress?
A. No; they have power to make all the Laws for a certain District, not more than ten miles square, where Congress meets, and where the Chief Officers of Government reside.This is called the Seat of Government.

Q. Has this District a Legislature of its own choice, as the States have?
A. No.

Q. Is it a part of any State?
A. No. It consists of territory, which the States have given up, for the express purpose that it might be the seat of the General Government. The territory at present used for this purpose, is called the District of Columbia; and has been ceded, (that is, given up) by the States of Maryland and Virginia, within which it before lay.

Q. Is there any other place in the United States, which is thus ruled by Congress alone?
A. Yes all Forts, Magazines, (that is, places where powder and other things used by an army are laid up) Arsenals, (that is, buildings where arms are kept) and Dock-yards; (that is, places where vessels of war are built) which belong to the United States, are governed,not by the Legislatures of the States in which they may be, but by the General Government alone.

Q. What other power is conferred by the Constitution upon the Congress of the United States?
A. A very large and general authority, "to make all laws which shall be necessary and proper for carrying into execution the foregoing powers", (that is, all the powers of which we have been speaking) "and all other powers vested by the Constitution in the Government of the United States, or in any department or officer thereof". Thus, for example, when the Constitution says, that Congress may coin money, that gives Congress power to make all the laws necessary to determine what the coin shall be how they shall be marked of what metal they shall be made what shall be their weight what shall be their value where they shall be made what buildings shall be erected for the purpose how many persons shall be employed what their duty shall be what pay they shall receive what account they shall keep what security they shall give, and how

they shall be punished if they neglect their duty. It is the same with every other power given by the Constitution; if its execution requires a hundred different laws, Congress may pass them all.

Q, May slaves be imported, that is, brought into the United States?
A. No, whoever engages in the slave trade is a pirate.

Q. May slaves be held, that is, owned, and made to work by citizens of the United States?
A. Yes.

Q. If they escape from one State into another, may the State into which they flee set them at liberty?
A. No.

Q. Suppose any American citizen is seized and put in prison, may he be kept there as long as those who seized him think fit?
A. No; he may get a writ of Habeas Corpus.

Q. What is that?
A. It is a command from Court, by which the jailor is forced to allow the prisoner to be brought up before a Judge, that the cause of his being put in prison may be examined into; in order, that if there is no law to keep him there, he may immediately be set at liberty.

Q. Must this command be given whenever it is applied for?
A. Yes, except at certain times, when this privilege is suspended (that is, interrupted for a time, but not taken away).

Q. When may this right of having a writ of Habeas Corpus, which belongs by the Constitution to every citizen, be suspended?
A. Only in cases of rebellion by our own citizens, or invasion of the country by an enemy; when the public danger is so great as to require persons to be kept in prison, who might otherwise be set at liberty. As soon as this extreme danger is past, the right of Habeas Corpus must be immediately restored.

Q. Is this a very great and important privilege, and ought all Americans to guard it with the greatest care?
A. It is one of the greatest rights of a freeman and Americans must never surrender it,under any pretext, if they value and would preserve their liberty.

Q. May a man's children be punished by law for his offence?
A. In some countries, where a man has been guilty of treason, (that is, making war against the Government) a law is passed called a bill of attainder, by which his children are prevented from being, heirs to him or to any other person; and, if he belonged to what in those countries is called the nobility, and his children would have belonged to it too,they are prevented; nor can they nor their children, nor their children's children, recover this privilege, till an act is passed for that purpose. No such law can be made in this country; it is expressly forbidden by the Constitution.

Q. May a citizen of the United States be punished for doing what, when he did it, was not forbidden by any law, but against which a law was passed afterwards?
A. No. A law that attempts to punish actions that were done before the law was made, is called an "ex-post-facto law". This also is expressly forbidden by the Constitution.

Q. When a direct tax is laid, that is, when Congress orders that a certain sum of money must be paid by each citizen, for the public use, what is the rule by which it is to be collected?
A. The census, or public counting of the people.

Q. May any money be required to be paid on goods exported, (that is, carried out) from any of the States?
A. No.

Q. May any law be passed giving to the ports of one State, (that is, the places where vessels arrive and depart with goods) a preference over those of another, so that goods coming to some ports, shall have less duties to pay to Government than the same goods coming to other ports?
A. No.

Q. May vessels coming from sea with goods which they wish to deliver in one State, be obliged to land those goods, or to enter them, that is, give an account of them at the Custom-house, or to pay the duties on them in another State?
A. No.

Q. When a vessel leaves the ports of one State with goods which she is carrying to sea,can she be obliged to dear those goods, that is, give an account of them at the Custom-house, in another State?
A. No; each State may carry on its own commerce without the interference of any other State.

Q. In what way can the money of the United States be drawn out of the Treasury (or place where it is kept)?
A. It can be drawn out only by authority of a law of Congress; and such a law is called an Appropriation.

Q. Must a full account be kept of all moneys received into the Treasury, and paid out of it; and must this account be published, that is, printed and sold from time to time?
A. Yes

Q. You said that in some countries, a part of the people are called Nobility; what does that mean?
A. Almost all Europe was once under the power of Rome, and formed part of what was called the Roman Empire. This Empire was attacked, overrun, and at last conquered entirely, by a hardy set of people who came from the north in vast numbers. These people were commanded by their chiefs or kings; and when the countries which they invaded gave up fighting, and yielded every thing to the conquerors, the whole of the land was divided into portions and given by the king to his chief officers, who divided it again among their followers. These great officers were called by various names or titles, as Dukes, Earls, Counts, etc. and when they died, their oldest sons were called by the same titles; which continued in this manner to descend in certain great and rich families. It is these families which are now known in most countries of Europe as Nobles, or the Nobility and they have great privileges over the other citizens.

Q. Can any families be thus distinguished from the rest in this Republic?
A. No; no title of Nobility can be granted here. The only titles among us, are those which mark a person's trade in the army or navy, or his office in the State.

Q. May any citizen of the United States receive a title of nobility from the king, or prince,or government of any other country?
A. The Government does not interfere with private persons but no person holding any office of profit or trust under the republic can accept of either a title, sum of money as salary, an office, or even a present, from any such prince or government, without the express consent of Congress.

Q. Why is this?
A. To guard against any foreign prince getting influence over those who are in power among us, by bribery of any kind; a title would be a better bribe to some men than money.

Q. You said that when the states entered into that agreement by which they set up a General Government over them all, they had each a perfect right to govern themselves as free, sovereign and independent States: and that they gave up a part of their power to the General Government, and kept the rest of it in their own Lands. What are the powers which they gave up?
A.The power of making treaties (that is, bargains or agreements with other nations)alliances, (that is, agreements with some other country, that the two shall help each other,in something they wish to accomplish, or in avoiding some common danger); and confederations (that is agreements among several different countries that they shall all join together in some object for their common benefit). None of these acts can now be performed by any one of the states, separately, but must be done only for the whole by the General Government.

Q. What other powers did they give up?
A.The right to grant letters of marque and reprisal: the right to coin money; (both these have been explained) the right to emit bills of credit; (that is, issue printed promises to pay certain sums of money on the credit of the state, the same as a Bank issues Bank notes), to make any thing but gold and silver a lawful tender in the payment of debts.

Q. What does that mean?
A. When one man owes another, and goes to him and offers him money to the full amount of his debt, that is called a tender; (or offer); and if the money is such as the law says shall pass, it is a lawful tender; and if the man refuses it, he can never sue the other for that debt, nor is the debtor obliged to pay it. Now, though money is commonly made of gold and silver, yet sometimes a Government may make a law by which certain printed notes are to pass the same as gold and silver; and after such a law, that kind of printed notes are a lawful tender to pay debts with. (This kind of paper was issued by Congress in our revolution). The states, by the Constitution, gave up the power to do this, and now it can be done by the General Government only.

Q. Did the states give up any other power?
A. They are forbidden by the Constitution, in the same manner that Congress is, to pass any bill of attainder, or ex-post-facto law, or grant any title of nobility, nor can they make any law which shall "impair the obligation of contracts".

Q. What does that mean?
A. It means that when a bargain has been made between any two parties, by which one agrees and binds himself to do some particular thing not then forbidden by law, the state in which

this agreement, or contract, was made shall not afterwards make any law by which the person who thus bound himself shall be set free from any part of that bargain without the consent of the other party, with whom he made the contract.

Q. What else are the states forbidden to do?
A. They cannot lay any duty on exports or imports.

Q. May they not lay enough duty to pay for the expenses of collecting the duties laid by Congress?
A. Yes, but no more; and if more is received than is wanted for this use, it must be paid into the Treasury of the United States.

Q. May any of the States lay a tonnage duty; that is, require a sum of money to be paid by every vessel entering any of the harbors in that State?
A. No.

Q. May they keep soldiers whom they pay, in time of peace?
A. No.

Q. May they keep ships of war, in time of peace?
A. No.

Q. May one State enter into an agreement with another State?
A. No.

Q. May they make a treaty or agreement with any other nation?
A. No.

Q. May they make war?
A. No; not unless an enemy has entered their bounds, or is in such danger of entering,that there is no time to wait for the aid of the General Government.

Q. Why did the States give up all these powers?
A. Because they could be better protected by one powerful Government ruling over the mall united than they could have been, if they had remained separate; and, if they would have such a Government, they must consent each to give up a part of their own power, in order to make it; if the General Government had no power, it would be of no use.

Q. Who executes the laws which Congress have made, that is, who takes care that every body shall obey the laws?
A. The President of the United States.

Q. Can he make the law?
A. Not at all. These two powers, of making law, and executing law, are kept by the Constitution, entirely separate; the power that makes the law cannot execute it, and the power that executes the law cannot make it. The one of these powers is called the Legislative, and the other is called the Executive power.

Q. Is there any advantage in this?
A. Certainly; it is the great safeguard of freedom because, if the one makes oppressive laws, the other may refuse to execute them; or, if the one wishes to do tyrannical acts, the other may refuse to make a law for them.

Q. How does any man become President of the United States?
A. He is elected [chosen] by the people of the United States.

Q. How is this done; do the people themselves at once choose the President?
A. No; this might lead to great confusion. But the people choose the Legislatures of the different States, these Legislatures appoint electors, and those electors choose the President.

Q. Explain this more particularly.
A. You know what is meant by the Legislatures of the States; they consist of persons chosen in each State to make the State laws. These persons, when met together, appoint,in any way they think proper, a number of persons who are called Electors, because they afterwards choose the President.

Q. How many of these Electors of President are appointed in each State?
A. As many as the state has members in both Houses of Congress. For instance; a state which is entitled to two Senators and eight members of the House of Representatives must appoint ten electors of President; a state which has two Senators and twenty members of the House of Representatives, must appoint twenty-two electors.

Q. May any person they please be appointed an elector?
A. Not every person may; Senators of the United States, members of the House of Representatives, and all persons who hold any office of trust or profit under the United States, are incapable of being electors of the President.

Q. Why?
A. For fear any President of the United States might use improper means to get himself chosen again when his time of service should expire. The President has frequent opportunities

to see the members of Congress and persuade them; and as he himself has the appointment of most persons who hold offices, he might threaten to remove, or promise to keep them in their places, and thus destroy their freedom of election.

Q. How do these electors proceed?
A. The electors appointed by each state meet in the states that appointed them, and vote by ballot for the President, and for another officer called the Vice President of the United States. The electors all meet on one and the same day in their several states; the day is fixed by Congress.

Q. What do you mean by voting by ballot?
A. When it is wished to conceal the manner in which each particular person voted, and yet to know what is the opinion of the greater number of voters, the voters instead of speaking their minds, put each a piece of folded paper into a box; these papers are called ballots, and when all have voted, these ballots are examined and counted.

Q. May both the persons whom the electors of any state vote for, as President and Vice President, be natives of that state in which they are voted for?
A. No; only one of them; the other must be a native of some other state.

Q. How do they distinguish which of the persons is voted for as President and which as Vice President?
A. The ballots are taken separately, on different pieces of paper, and it is besides written on the ballot — whether the person is voted for as the one or as the other. Separate lists are kept in which they put down the names of all the persons who are voted for, either as President or as Vice President, and the number of votes given for each; these lists are signed by the

electors, and then sealed up and sent to the seat of government directed to the President of the Senate. For the greater security, two copies are made, one of them is sent by the mail, and another by a messenger, sent for the express purpose of carrying it.

Q. What does the President of the Senate do with these lists?
A. He opens them in the presence of the Senate and the House of Representatives, who are all met in one hall to be present when the votes are counted. Each House appoints some of its own members who unite in a committee and count all the votes; when the person having the greatest number of votes for President is declared to be the President,and he who has the most votes for Vice President is declared Vice President of the United States.

Q. Suppose no one person has a majority (that is more than half) of all the votes for President, is the person who has the most votes considered as chosen?
A. No.

Q. What is done in that case?
A. The House of Representatives immediately proceeds to choose, by ballot, from those persons, not more than three, who stand the highest on the list of votes for President, one to be President of the United States.

Q. Are they bound to choose the person who has most votes?
A. No; they may take either one of those three persons who have the most votes.

Q. Do they vote, on this occasion, in a different manner from what they do on all other occasions?
A. Yes; in choosing the President they vote, not by single members, but by States; that is,each State has one vote only, whether its Representatives are many or few; and a majority of the whole number of States is necessary to a choice.

Q. Must all the States vote?
A. All may vote if they are present and desire it; but if only two thirds of the States vote, the election is good .

Q. Suppose the House of Representatives cannot, or does not, choose any one, must there be no President?
A. In that case, the Vice President must perform the duty of President.

Q. If neither of the persons voted for by the Electors as Vice President has a majority of all their votes, what is done?
A.The Senate then chooses one of the two persons who have the most votes. A majority of the whole number of Senators is necessary to the choice, but two thirds of their number is sufficient to vote.

Q. May any person be chosen President of the United States?
A. Not every person; none may be chosen unless he has been born in the United States, or was a citizen when the Constitution Was agreed to, nor can such a one be chosen if he is less than thirty-five years old, or if he has not resided within the United States for fourteen years.

Q. May any person be chosen Vice President?
A. No one may be chosen as Vice President who is forbidden by the above rule to be chosen as President.

Q. If the President of the United States should die, or should be put out of office, or should resign his office, or should from any cause be unable to do the duties which belong to it, what is to be done?
A. His duties must then be performed by the Vice President.

Q. But suppose the same thing should have happened to the Vice President also?
A. Then the Congress must declare by law who shall perform the duties till another President is chosen, or till the President is again able to perform them himself.

Q. Does the President receive any thing for his services?
A. The honor of filling so high and honorable a station by the choice of a great and free people, and the glory of leaving his name in their history as the faithful friend and father of his country, is, of itself, enough to fill the wishes of the most aspiring mind, and no doubt the place would be sought as eagerly as it now is, though not a dollar should be given to the man who fills it; but because his station exposes him to great expenses he is allowed a salary sufficient to meet them.

Q. What is the amount of the President's salary, that is, the sum of money paid him by the United States every year?
A. It is at present fixed at twenty-five thousand dollars.

Q. May he receive any other money from the United States, or from any one State?
A. No; he is expressly forbidden to receive any other sum of money than his salary.

Q. Why?
A. Lest, if any State allowed him money, he might be led to favor that State more than the others; and lest, if he was suffered to receive other sums from the United States, he might amass so much money as should make him a dangerous citizen to a free country.

Q. Does the President take any oath before he enters upon his office?
A. Yes.

Q. What is an oath?
A. It is a solemn calling upon God, who knows the hearts of all men, and will call everyman to account for his conduct in this world, to bear witness that what a man says is true,or that what he promises he means to perform.

Q. What is the President's oath of office?
A. It is in these words "I do solemnly swear, that I will faithfully execute the office of President of the United States; and will, to the best of my ability, preserve, protect, and defend the Constitution of the United States."

Q. What are the powers which belong to the President?
A. He is commander in chief, both of the army and navy; every officer of both, from the highest to the lowest, is obliged to obey his orders.

Q. Are the officers of the militia obliged to obey them?
A. Yes, whenever the militia are called out in the service of the United States; (at other times they are under the command of the Governors of their own States).

Q. Has he any other powers?
A. Yes; he may grant reprieves and pardons for offences against the United States.

Q. What is a reprieve?
A. When a person has been tried, found guilty, and condemned to be punished on a certain day, a reprieve is a putting off of the punishment to some other time.

Q. What is a pardon?
A. It is the delivering of a condemned person from the punishment of his offence. A reprieve only delays punishment; a pardon prevents it entirely.

Q. May the President do this in all cases of offences against the United States?
A. In all cases, except cases of impeachment.

Q. What other powers has he?
A. He has a very solemn power, that of making Treaties for the United States with other nations.

Q. Why is this so solemn a power?
A. Because a treaty is the supreme law of the land, and usually concerns matters of great importance to us all.

Q. Is nobody joined with the President in this power? Or may he make any agreement he thinks fit, with other nations?
A. This power is so great and weighty, that the Constitution will entrust it to no one man.Even the President cannot make a treaty without the consent of the Senate of the United States; nor is it sufficient that a majority of the Senate agree to it; two thirds of all the Senators who are present when the vote is taken, must agree to any treaty, before it is binding on the United States.

Q. Has the President any other power?
A. Yes; powers of nomination and appointment.

Q. What do you mean by this?
A. When persons are to be employed to do the duties of certain great public offices, none can be so employed but those whom the President first nominates; that is, proposes to the Senate, and whom the Senate consent to have employed; and when the Senate has given this consent, the persons cannot act in their office till they receive orders to do so from the President; such an order is called their appointment, and when put in writing it is called their commission.

Q. What officers are appointed in this manner?
A. Ambassadors and foreign Ministers; (that is, persons sent by the United States to the Government of some other nation, either to prepare some public treaty, or to reside there as the representative of this country). Consuls, (persons sent by this country to reside in the ports of other nations, to protect our commerce; that is, to see that our vessels, our sailors, and the property of our merchants, are properly treated there, according to the treaties and laws of both countries). Judges of the Supreme Court, and all other officers of the United States, except those who are expressly ordered by the Constitution to be appointed by some other person than the President.

Q. May the President appoint any officer without the consent of the Senate?
A. Yes, if Congress makes a law giving him the power; but this applies only to inferior officers, that is, such as have other officers over them.

Q. May Congress give the appointment of such officers to any other than the President?
A. Yes; it may give it to the Courts of Law, or to the Heads of Departments.

Q. What do you mean by the Heads of Departments?
A. This name is given to certain officers who have the chief care under the President, of the four great branches of the Government, called the Executive Departments ; and who are called the Secretary of State, the Secretary of the Treasury, the Secretary of War, and the Secretary of the Navy.

Q. Are the duties of these officers declared by the Constitution?
A. No; but by a law of Congress. They are, however, persons of great importance in our government. The Secretary of State attends to every thing which concerns our affairs with other nations; and also to those the General Government with the Governments of the different States; the Secretary of the Treasury attends to all that concerns the money of the United States; the Secretary of War manages the business of the army; and the Secretary of the Navy that which concerns our vessels of war. All these officers are, however, under the control of the President; he may require their opinion in writing on any subject that belongs to their different departments, but he is not bound by it; he may also dismiss them from office.

Q. Suppose any of the officers whom the President has appointed by the consent of the Senate should die, or should resign his office, while the Senate is not sitting; what is to be done?
A. The President may appoint another person in his place who shall hold the office till the end of the next meeting of the Senate.

Q. What are the duties of the President?
A. He must from time to time give information to Congress of the state of the United States.

Q. Does he know what is the state of the nation better than the Members of Congress?
A. Yes; his office is such that he has a better opportunity of knowing it. Each Member of Congress resides only in one State, but the President resides at a spot in the middle of them all. It is the duty of all officers below him, to send reports of the various affairs in which they are employed, to one or other of the Heads of Departments, and these lay all the knowledge they thus obtain, before the President direction and assistance in the many and great duties he has to perform. He is, therefore, of all other persons, best acquainted with the general concerns of this nation.

Q. When does he lay this information before Congress?
A. He makes a very full statement of it when they first meet, in what is usually called the President's Speech; and from time to time, while the two Houses are met, he sends to each of them messages, in which he gives more particular statements than he could do in his first general speech.

Q. Suppose Congress wish to know from the President something which he has not told them in his speech or messages, may they call upon him to communicate it?
A. Yes, and if he does not think that the public good requires it to be kept secret, he always answers the call, and gives them the knowledge they desired, if he can do so.

Q. Does he do more than communicate information to the Congress?
A. Yes; his duty is also to recommend to them such things as he thinks will be for the advantage of the country.

Q. Are they obliged to do as he advises?
A. No. They pay respectful attention to what he says to them, and listen to the reasons he gives in favor of the measures he recommends, but they are at full liberty to follow their own judgement in ail cases.

Q. Is it to be desired that Congress should always comply with the advice of the President?
A. No; for then his advice would, in time, come to have the authority of a command; it would be the President and not Congress who made the laws; and the liberty of the country would be in the greatest danger. There is no more dangerous despot than one who can make his will obeyed, and yet preserve the forms of a free government. Augustus Caesar ruled the whole Roman Empire with absolute sway, yet did every thing by resolves of the Senate, as if Rome was free.

Q. Suppose some very important matter should happen while Congress is not met, can the President call them together?
A. Yes. He can call either both Houses, or only one; if any law is to be made, both Houses must be called; if only a treaty or an appointment is to be made, the Senate only need be assembled.

Q. Suppose, when both Houses are met, they should find themselves unable to agree about the time at which they will adjourn, (that is, cease to meet) can the President end the dispute?
A. Yes, by adjourning both Houses.

Q. In that case, when are they to meet again?
A. At any time the President fixes, when he adjourns them.

Q. What other duty is required of the President?
A. He must receive all ambassadors and foreign ministers; that is, persons sent by other nations to make treaties with us, or to reside here as representatives of their own government.

Q. Has he any other duty?
A. Yes, he has one great, general, and constant duty in which all this power is put at his command, it is to take care that the laws shall be faithfully executed; that is, that whatever Congress orders shall be done, and that whoever disobeys the laws shall be punished.

Q. May he be punished himself?
A. We have already seen that every civil officer of the United States may be impeached by the House of Representatives, tried before the Senate, and, if guilty, may be turned out of office. The crimes for which this is done are chiefly treason and bribery. Treason, we said, is making war against the United States, by endeavoring to resist or overturn the government; bribery means the unlawful taking of money by an officer for doing or omitting some act of his office.

Q. Does not every officer receive money for doing the duties of his office?
A. Yes, the law allows him a certain sum; but a bribe is something more than this, given him not by the United States, but by somebody who wishes him to favor them in the exercise of his power as a public officer. It is wicked to offer a bribe, it is still worse to accept one.

Q. Can there be no bribery but by means of money?
A. Yes; bribes may be offered in various shapes; any benefit or advantage offered to an officer for an improper end is a bribe.

Q. What do you understand by a Court?
A. A place where a Judge sits to hear and determine causes according to law.

Q. Are Courts necessary?
A. Certainly. Wherever laws are made there must be some way of determining when they have been disobeyed, and of causing those who disobey them to be punished. This is the use of a Court and of a Judge. When one person believes that another has broken the laws, to his injury, or to the injury of the public, he may cause that person to appear before a Judge and have it determined by witnesses, whether he has broken the laws or not; and if he has, he is forced to suffer such a punishment as the law directs.

Q. Are there Courts in every State of the United States?
A. Yes. Each State appoints Judges of its own to see that its laws are executed.

Q. Are there also other Courts belonging to no particular State but to the United States?
A. Yes.

Q. Are all these Courts equal, or is one superior to another?
A. They are not all equal but in each State some of the State Courts are set over others;and so it is with the Courts of the United States.

Q. Why are they not all equal?
A. Some are set over others, in order, that if one makes any mistake it may be corrected by that above it. When a citizen

thinks he has been wronged in a lower Court, he may take his cause to a higher one; this is called an appeal; and if in this higher Court, he still thinks he is wronged, he may appeal to a court higher still, until he has got to the highest Court in his own State.

Q. Can he take his cause from the State Courts to the Courts of the United States?
A. No; not unless his cause has to do with a law made by a State, which as he supposes is contrary to the Constitution of the United States. That question can be settled only by the Supreme Court of the United States.

Q. Suppose his cause has to do with a law of the United States and not a State law?
A. He must go at once to the Courts of the United States.

Q. What are these?
A. They consist of one Supreme Court, (the highest of all), and of such other Courts,under this, as Congress may from time to time establish.

Q. Has Congress established any?
A. Yes it has appointed some which are called Circuit Courts of the United States; and others, below these, which are called District Courts of the United States.

Q. What Judges sit in the Circuit Courts of the United States?
A. The Judges of the United States Supreme Court.

Q. What Judges sit in the District Courts of the United States?
A. District Judges.

Q. What kind of causes are tried in the Courts of the United States?
A. Any cause must be tried there in which the dispute is about the true meaning of any part of the Constitution.

Q. What else?
A. All causes under the laws of the United States.

Q. Any others?
A. Yes; all which depend upon treaties between the United States and other nations.

Q. What other causes?
A. All in which Ambassadors or other public Ministers, or Consuls, sent to the United States by other governments, are parties concerned.

Q. What others?
A. All causes which concern the taking or detaining of ships at sea, and all which concern crimes committed at sea, or in harbors, or rivers or in forts and dock-yards, belonging to the United States.

Q. What other causes are tried in these Courts?
A. All disputes in which the United States is a party; all disputes between one State and another State; all in which one of the States sues any person that is the citizen of another of the States; all in which a citizen of one State sues a citizen of another State; all in which citizens of one and the same State lay claim to land under grants of different States; all in which one of the States sues a citizen of some foreign country; and all in which citizens of the United States, and citizens of any other country sue each other. But not where citizens of one State sue another State; or where citizens or subjects of a foreign State sue one of the States of the Union.

Q. Must all causes of these several kinds be begun in one of the inferior courts of the United States, or may any of them be commenced at once in the Supreme Court?
A. All cases which have to do with ambassadors, public ministers, and consuls; and all those in which one of the States is a party, may be begun in the Supreme Court; the others, after being commenced in the inferior Courts of the United States, may be removed to the Supreme Court by an appeal; but this is submitted to the regulation of Congress, who may determine by law when it may be done, and in what manner.

Q. How are the Judges of the Courts of the United States appointed?
A. By the President, with the advice and consent of the Senate.

Q. How long do they remain in office?
A. During good behavior; that is, until they resign their office or are turned out of it for some great offence.

Q. Why are not Judges elected from time to time, like Members of the House of Representatives and Senators? And why may they not be removed from their offices unless they are proved to be guilty of great offences?
A. If Judges held their places at the mere good pleasure of the people, they would be greatly tempted to act in a partial and improper manner in order to please those who chose them to office, and to keep their favor; but when they know that no man or number of men can turn them out of office so long as they do their duty, they administer justice without fear and with an equal regard to all who ask it.

Q. Why then should not Legislators hold their office in the same way?
A. Because they make the laws, while Judges only explain and apply them; it would be very dangerous to liberty to give our law makers power for life; they require restraint lest they should become our tyrants; therefore their time of office is made short, so that if the people think them unwise or unfaithful they may refuse to give them the office again.

Q. You said that the use of Courts was to determine when the laws have been disobeyed,and causing those who have disobeyed them to be punished. How do Courts answer this end?
A. When a person is charged with having done something to his neighbor, or to the State,which is forbidden by law, the fact is judged of by a Jury.

Q. What do you mean by a Jury?
A. A company of citizens, chosen by lot, and who have no interest in the matter, who listen to the proofs brought against the person accused, and who then agree among themselves whether the accusation has been proved or not. When they declare this agreement in opinion, it is called their verdict; and according to this, the cause is decided.

Q. Is this a wise regulation?
A. Certainly. The trial by jury, is a most precious privilege as it secures to every man a fair hearing, and is the best safe-guard of his liberty, property, and life; all which might be taken from him by a partial or corrupt Judge, if that officer alone had to decide on the guilt or innocence of those who are tried before him.

Q. Does a Jury decide in civil suits as well as in criminal prosecutions?
A. I do not understand the difference between them.

Q. By a civil suit, I mean one citizen's calling another into court to answer him for some injury committed against him; by a criminal prosecution, I mean a citizen's being brought up by a public accuser for some crime committed against society at large, and for which he is liable to public punishment.
A. A jury decides in both cases. When an officer of the United States is impeached, the accuser is the House of Representatives, and the jury is the Senate; but in ordinary prosecutions and suits, the jury consists of twelve persons, residing near the place where the act was committed.

Q. May an accused person be tried in a different State from that where the criminal act was committed?
A. No.

Q. Suppose the act was committed at sea, or in some other place not within any one of the States of the Union, where must the trial be held?
A. Where Congress shall have appointed by law.

Q. Ought all the public acts of a State, and of all its courts and officers, to be recorded in writing?
A. Certainly; not only to preserve a remembrance of them, but that those persons who are affected by these acts may be able to show proof of them, and if injured, to obtain redress.

Q. When such a record is made in one of the States, and a copy of it, duly proved, is given, must that record be received as proof by all the other States?
A. Yes. But Congress may determine by law in what manner the record shall be proved for this purpose.

Q. When a citizen of one State goes into any other State of the Union, may he be treated as if he was a foreigner? Or may any difference be made between his privileges and those of the citizens of that State?
A.No. He shall enjoy every privilege which they do.

Q. If a person charged with a crime in one State, shall flee from justice into the bounds of another State is he safe from pursuit and trial?
A. No. If the Governor of the State where the crime was committed applies to the Governor of the State where he has taken refuge, the latter shall cause him to be delivered up.

Q. Suppose a slave in one State shall run away from his master, and flee into another State, does he thereby become free?
A. No. On application of his master, and proof of his being a slave, he must be given up.

Q. How many States were there which revolted from Great Britain at the Revolution?
A. Thirteen.

Q. Did they all agree to the Federal Constitution at the time it went into operation?
A. Not all, but the rest came in soon after.

Q. Was it then expected that other States would be formed and join the Union?
A. Yes, and provision was made for admitting them.

Q. By whom were they to be admitted?
A. By Congress.

Q. Is their number limited?
A. No.

Q. Or their population?
A. Not by the Constitution; but Congress has determined that a district or territory containing sixty thousand inhabitants may be received into the Union as a State.

Q. Then that number of people in any of the States may be erected into a new State?
A. No. No new State can be formed within the limits of a State already formed.

Q. May two States be united by Congress into one: or parts of two States be erected into a third State?
A. Not unless the Legislatures of both such States give their consent.

Q. When the Colonies separated from Great Britain was their territory all peopled?
A. No; large tracts of land in several of the States, remained in its natural, wild state.

Q. When the States united under the Constitution, what was done with these wild lands?
A. They were given up by the several States that owned them, and set apart as common property, for the good of the whole.

Q. Who has power to govern these territories as they become settled? And to sell the land to settlers?
A. The Congress of the United States.

Q. Have they since been extensively settled?
A. Yes. Many new States have been formed within their limits, and many more are expected to be. They are in the mean while divided into several distinct portions called territories, each of which has a form of government suited to its amount of population,and a Delegate in Congress with power to speak, but not to vote in that body.

Q. Has any State the right to set up a monarchical form of government for itself, that is a government where the supreme power is in the hands of a king?
A. No. When the Colonies united they were all republics, the new government they formed for the Union was republican, and they then secured to every State which had joined or should join the confederation, a republican form of government.

Q. Who is to see that this regulation is carried into effect?
A. The Congress.

Q. Does Congress secure any other privilege to the different States?
A. Yes. It must protect them from invasion by an enemy. This is one of the most important benefits of our Union; each State has the protection of the whole.

Q. Should unruly persons in any of the States attempt by violence to resist and overturn the State Government, and should they gain such strength that that State is not able to quell them, must Congress interfere?
A. Yes, if applied to by the Governor or Legislature of such State. But not to prevent a peaceable alteration of the laws attempted in a regular and proper manner.

Q. The majority of the people of any State may certainly alter its laws, provided they do not violate the Constitution: but may the Constitution itself be altered?
A. Yes. The Constitution being nothing more than an expression of the will of the people of the United States, is at all times within their own power, and they may change it as they like, but it ought not to be changed till it is very clearly shown to be the wish of the people.

Q. How is this to be found out?
A. When two thirds of the members both of the Senate and of the House of Representatives shall agree in opinion that an alteration would be proper, they may state such alteration and propose it to be considered by the people of all the States. The alteration must then be considered by the Legislature of each of the States, or by a Convention in each State, (which is a meeting of persons chosen by the people for this particular purpose); and if three fourths of the States agree to the amendment, it then becomes a part of the Constitution.

Q. But if three fourths of the States should thus agree to an amendment which would deprive the remaining States against their will of their equal vote in the Senate, would such amendment be binding?
A. No. This case is provided against in the Constitution, and one other (in relation to slaves) which could only happen

previous to the year 1808; but as that year is now past,no farther notice need be taken of it.

Q. What is the supreme law of the United States?
A. The Constitution itself is supreme; and all laws and treaties made by Congress and the President, in conformity with it, are superior to any law made by one of the States, so that if the law of a State contradicts a law of Congress, the State law is of no force, and the United States law alone must be obeyed.

Q. What security have we that the Constitution will be observed?
A. The President, the Members of Congress, the Members of all the State Legislatures,and all public officers of the United States, and of each one of the States, takes an oath,when they enter upon their several offices, to obey the Constitution. But the great security for its observance lies in the wisdom and excellence of the Constitution itself, and the conviction of the whole people of the United States, that it is for their true interest to observe it inviolate. It has been tried for fifty years, and has done more to render this nation peaceable, powerful and happy than any form of government that ever existed among men.

Q. You said that the Constitution, however wise or good, might nevertheless be amended if the people of the United States chose?
A. Yes; the Constitution says so expressly.

Q. Has it ever been amended?
A. Yes, several times.

Q. What was the subject of the first amendment?
A. The subject of religious freedom.

Q. What do you mean by that?
A. I mean the right every man has to worship God in such way as he thinks fit, without being called to account for his opinions, or punished for them.

Q. Is this a sacred right, which ought to be guarded with the greatest care?
A. Certainly. God alone is the Judge of our religious belief and service, and no man has aright to interfere with it, so long as it does not lead us to injure or disturb our neighbor. A great part of the misery and oppression which has existed in the world, began with forcing men to do what their conscience disapproved.

Q. What amendment was made in the Constitution on this subject?
A. Congress was forbidden to make any law respecting an establishment of religion; that is, giving the preference to any one form of religion above another, and making laws to support it; or making laws to prevent men from freely holding or observing any particular form of religious belief and practice.

Q. Was any other subject introduced into the same amendment?
A. Yes; the freedom of speech and the freedom of the press.

Q. What do you understand by these expressions?
A. In a free country like ours, every citizen has a right to express his opinion of the character and conduct of our rulers, and of the laws they make for our government; to forbid this, or punish it, would be highly dangerous to our liberty. If those chosen by their fellow citizens to rule the State, rule in a

foolish or wicked manner, it ought to be known,that they may be speedily turned out of office; but if nobody might find fault with them without danger of punishment, their bad conduct would never be exposed, and they might continue in power to the great injury of us all. The right to speak our opinions is the freedom of speech; and the right to print them, that they may be read by others, is the freedom of the press.

Q. But suppose I say of my rulers what is false and injurious, may I not be punished?
A. Yes, if they can prove in a court of justice that what you have said is false, and that your saying or publishing it has injured them. So may any of your fellow citizens. But you are still at liberty to speak and to print, being liable to the consequences if you abuse your liberty.

Q. If the people shall be of opinion that any of the acts of their rulers have been wrong,may they meet together to petition, that is publicly to ask, that these acts may be altered?
A. Yes, if they meet peaceably; but if they behave in a riotous or disorderly manner, they may, and ought to be punished.

Q. May they meet with arms in their hands?
A. Yes; the right to keep and to carry arms is one which belongs to the citizens at all times; but arms must not be used except to support the laws or to resist the enemy.

Q. As the public safety requires that the Government should employ hired soldiers, as well as the militia, may these soldiers be sent to live in the house of any citizen and at his expense, without his consent?
A. Never, when the nation is at peace. When it is at war, it may often be necessary to do this; but the Constitution declares that even then, it must only be done according to law;

not according to the mere good pleasure of an officer of the army, but in a manner which the Representatives of the people shall lay down.

Q. Has the Government power to enter the house of a citizen and search it, and to take him, and his papers, and his property, at any time it thinks fit?
A. No. It is sometimes necessary and proper to seize a man's person and property, and to search his papers; but this may never be done, until some of his fellow citizens charge him with some offence which would require this to be done, make it appear probable that he is guilty, and swear to what they declare against him. Then a Judge gives to an officer a warrant to search or to seize ; but the warrant must say particularly what places are to be searched, and what persons or property is to be seized. Otherwise no man would be secure.

Q. Suppose I am accused by my neighbor of some crime which is punished with death,(these are called capital crimes) or which would render me infamous in society; must I be seized and tried because he has accused me?
A. No. You must be either confined or in another manner prevented from going away,until his accusation is laid before a number of your fellow citizens, called a Grand Jury,who swear to act fairly in the case. They hear your accuser and all the proof he has to bring against you, and if they think that he is wrong in supposing you guilty, and that his proof is not sufficient, they refuse to have you tried, and you are set at liberty. But if they think his proof is such that you ought to be tried, they deliver to the Court what is called a Bill of Indictment; that is, a paper setting forth the crime you are said to have done, and according to this you are tried. So that

no man can be put on his trial, till many impartial men think and swear that there is reason to believe he is guilty.

Q. Does what you have now said, apply to soldiers and sailors in the army and the fleet?
A. No; they are tried according to certain rules and regulations, called articles of war, to which they swear to submit when they become soldiers or sailors.

Q. Does it apply to citizens who are in the militia?
A. No, not when engaged in actual service, in time of war or public danger; they are then subject to the articles of war. It applies to them at all other times.

Q. What other rights are secured to an accused person?
A. Whoever is accused of a criminal offence, (that means an offence for which he is to be tried by the State) shall have a speedy and public trial. He may not be kept confined longer than is necessary, nor may he be tried in a secret place, but openly before all who choose to attend. And he shall have a Jury of impartial men to try him. (The trial by Jury has been already explained). The men who compose his jury must be of the same State,and of the same district where the offence is said to have been committed. He must be fully informed of the nature of the charge brought against him, and how it came to be made.

Q. Suppose he knows of persons who could prove him not guilty of the charge, but they live far off, or are unwilling to attend his trial, can he force them to come?
A. Yes. The Court will grant him a certain paper called a Writ of Subpoena, and send it by an officer, to every person he

wants as a witness in his favor; and such persons are obliged to come, or be heavily punished.

Q. Has he any other privilege?
A. Yes, he has a right to have the advice of a lawyer to aid him in his defence, and to plead his cause.

Q. Can he be forced to bear witness against himself?
A. No.

Q. If he is once tried and not found guilty, may he be again tried for the same offence?
A. If it is an offence, which if proved against him, would put him in danger of losing his life, or suffering any bodily injury, he may not.

Q. Are my life, liberty, and property guarded by the Constitution, so that no man is allowed to touch either of them, except according to the laws of the land?
A. They are.

Q. But if my property is wanted for a useful public object, may it not be taken from me?
A. Yes, but you must be paid the full value of it in money.

Q. Suppose I am sued by my neighbor, about some property, am I to have a Jury to try the cause?
A. Yes, if the amount in dispute is more than twenty dollars.

Q. You said that when a person is charged with a criminal offence, he must be confined, or otherwise prevented from going away, till a Grand Jury has heard the accusation and

proof against him. How else can he be restrained from going off, but by confining him?
A. By obliging him to bring forward persons who will become his Bail; that means, who will agree to forfeit a certain sum of money if he goes away and does not return to be tried.

Q. Who has power to say how much money they shall agree to forfeit?
A. The Judge, before whom the man is accused.

Q. May he fix any sum he pleases?
A. No. The sum is to be according to the nature of the crime, and the danger of the accused man's running away, but it may not be made so great as to be cruel or unjust.

Q. Are offences ever punished by a fine; that is, by obliging the offender to pay a sum of money?
A. Yes, but here the same rule applies. The sum must not be made out of proportion to the offence, and the circumstances of the offender.

Q. May a Judge contrive new punishments out of his own head, or order such as are not in common use for such offence as has been committed?
A. No.

Q. Because the Constitution only speaks of certain rights belonging to citizens of the United States, does it follow that the citizens have no rights but these?
A. By no means.

Q. Has the United States Government any power but such as is contained in the Constitution?
A. No.

Q. Have the different States of the Union all the powers which rightfully belong to a State, except those which are denied to them by the Constitution?

A. Yes. When the States united to form a constitution for their General Government, they agreed to give up to that government some of the powers they had before, and they set down in the Constitution what these powers were. All other powers they keep. The same thing is true respecting the people. All the powers they have not given up to the State Governments or to the General Government, they keep in their own hands.

CONCLUSION

And now, my young friends, having gone through a short, and I hope, clear and intelligible view of this Constitution, I have a few parting words to say to each one of you.

In the first place, consider how happy and how highly favored is our country, in having a system of government so wisely calculated to secure the life, liberty, and happiness of all its citizens. Had you lived or travelled in other parts of the world, you would be much more sensible of this, than you can possibly be without such an opportunity of comparing our lot with that of others. But, as your reading increases, particularly in history and in travels, you will be able to form a more just estimate of what you enjoy. When you read of the oppression which has been, and still is exercised, I do not say in Africa and Asia,whose inhabitants are but partially civilized but even in the most enlightened countries of Europe; under absolute monarchs, a proud and haughty nobility a worldly, selfish, and ambitious priesthood a vast and rapacious standing army, and a host of greedy officers of government; and then turn your eyes on your own happy home, a land where none of these evils has any place where the people first make the laws and then obey them where they can be oppressed by none, but where every man's person, property, and privileges are surrounded by the law, and sacred from every thing but justice and the public good;how can you be sufficiently grateful to a beneficent Providence, which has thus endowed our country with blessings equally rich and rare?

In the next place, remember that this precious Constitution, thus wise, thus just, is your birth-right. It has been earned for you by your fathers, who counselled much, labored long, and shed their dearest blood, to win it for their children. To them, it was the fruit of toil and danger to you, it is a gift. Do not slight it on that account, but prize it as you ought. It is yours, no human power can deprive you of it, but your own folly and wickedness. To undervalue, is one of the surest ways to lose it. Take pains to know what the Constitution is the more you study, the higher you will esteem it. The better you understand your own rights, the more likely you will be to preserve and guard them.

And, in the last place, my beloved young countrymen, your country's hope, her treasure,and one day to be her pride and her defense; remember that a constitution which gives to the people so much freedom, and entrusts them with so much power, rests for its permanency, on their knowledge and virtue. An ignorant people are easily betrayed, and a wicked people can never be ruled by the mild influence of their own laws. If you would be free if you would see your country grow in all that constitutes true greatness cultivate knowledge flee from vice. The virtuous citizen is the true noble. He who enlightens his understanding controls his passions feels for his country's honor rejoices in her prosperity steps forth to aid her in the hour of danger devotes to her advancement the fruits of his mind, and consecrates to her cause, his time, his property, and his noblest powers, such a man is one of God's nobility; he needs neither riband, nor star; his country knows and remembers his name; nor could any title add to its honor, or to his reward. We have seen such men among us; we hope to see many more.

And though the glory of giving to their country a Constitution as this, is what none but they have been so blessed as to enjoy, yet you succeed to a task, but one degree removed from it, that of preserving what they have committed to your virtue, unsullied and unimpaired.

Made in United States
Orlando, FL
10 June 2023

33993883R00050